Contents: Poems

Pictures Of The Author
A Day At The Beach
Anniversary
Barnegat Light
Books
Brother Photos
My Brother
Photos of Dianne & Family
Dianne
Dinner
Dreams
Earthquake
Eidolon (ghosts)
Family Picture
Family
First Choice
Hell and High Water
Hurricane
Pictures Of Family
Marriage
My Fair Lady
My Lost Love
Retirement
Sanibel
Silent Love
Sunrise
Stephanie Pictures
Stephanie
The Letter
The Man I Am Looking For
The Masked Ball
The Phone
Too Late
Undeclared Love
Walking In The Sunshine
Wine and Roses
Your Name

Copyright 2015 by Matilda Dianne Gonzalez
239-839-7253 Naples, Florida

poems

Aug 1956

By Garnet Mahaffey

A Day At The Beach

Chores are all finished for the day
Laundry done and put away
Floors scrubbed and dusting done
Heading to the beach for some fun.

Book and chair in hand
I walk the burning sand
To find the perfect spot
Where the sun is not too hot.

As I turn the pages of my book
My mind takes a backward look
To the days of long ago
When our love was all aglow.

We watched the sun as it set
Our love, vowing never to forget
A dirty trick life did play
The sands of time took you away.

Now my book lies open in the sand
My eyes are focused on a distant land
Looking to the skies above
Until the day I join my love

By Garnet Mahaffey

Anniversary

Twenty years ago today
Was the day we were wed
Although you have gone away
There is no one in your stead.

The years we spent together
Were happiness beyond belief
If I had my choice, I would rather
Have them than this grief.

Why you had to go from me
To that land so far away
Will always remain a mystery
But I hope to join you someday.

On this day of our anniversary
To meet you in that world above
Is my hope and fervent plea
Then we will be reunited in our love.

By Garnet Mahaffey

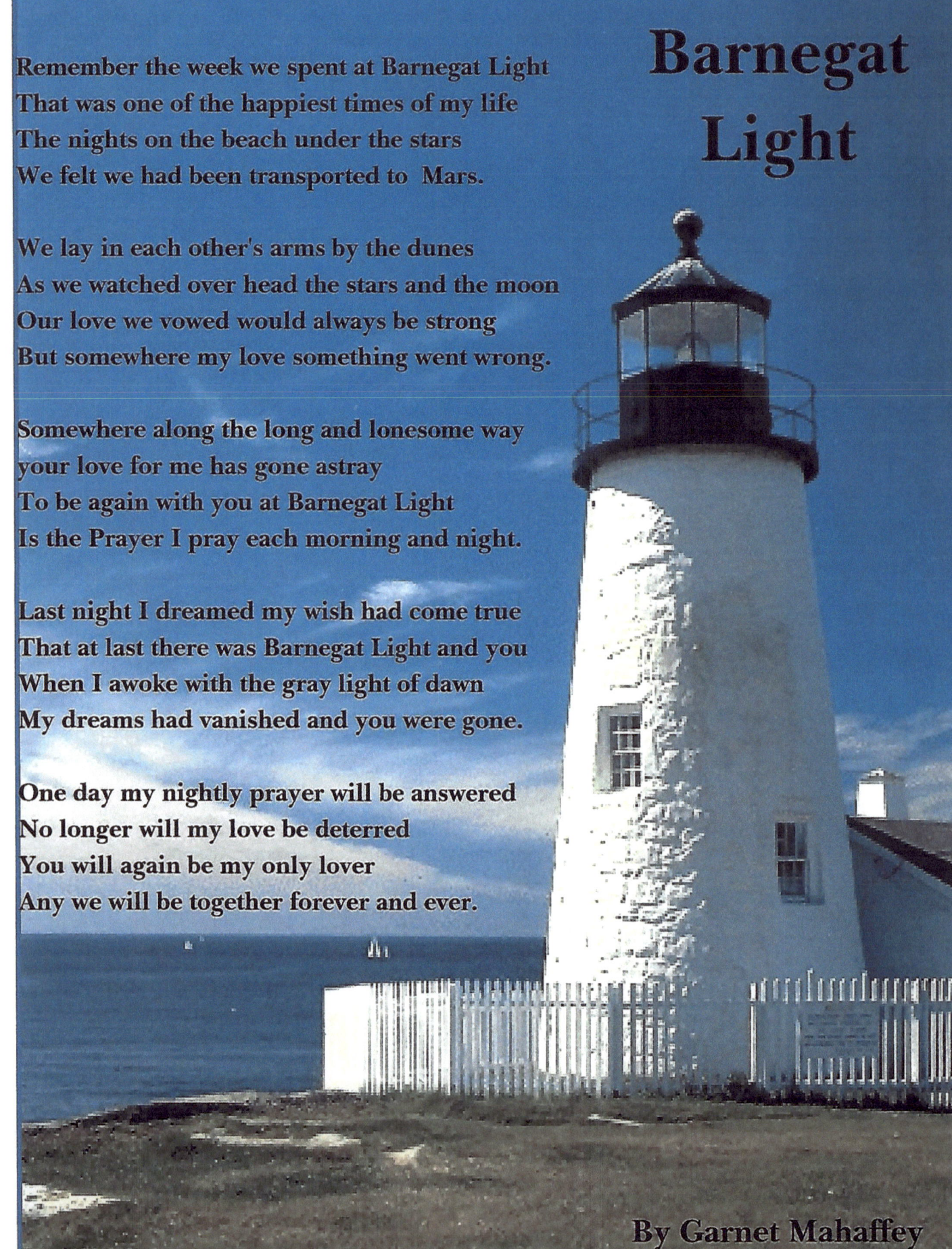

Barnegat Light

Remember the week we spent at Barnegat Light
That was one of the happiest times of my life
The nights on the beach under the stars
We felt we had been transported to Mars.

We lay in each other's arms by the dunes
As we watched over head the stars and the moon
Our love we vowed would always be strong
But somewhere my love something went wrong.

Somewhere along the long and lonesome way
your love for me has gone astray
To be again with you at Barnegat Light
Is the Prayer I pray each morning and night.

Last night I dreamed my wish had come true
That at last there was Barnegat Light and you
When I awoke with the gray light of dawn
My dreams had vanished and you were gone.

One day my nightly prayer will be answered
No longer will my love be deterred
You will again be my only lover
Any we will be together forever and ever.

By Garnet Mahaffey

Books

READING A BOOK LINE AFTER LINE
I LOOSE MYSELF IN ANOTHER TIME
THE ROUND TABLE KNIGHTS COME ALIVE
AS THEY FIGHT TO CLAIM THEIR PRIZE

LOVERS, I HAVE HAD MORE THAN A FEW
WHILE MY STACK OF BOOKS GREW
DUKES, EARLS AND ONCE A KING
PIRATES TO ME THEIR GOLD DO BRING.

I TRAVEL TO DISTANT SHORES
BACK IN TIME TO LANDS OF YORE
AND IN THE FUTURE TOO
I HAVE EVEN BEEN TO XANADU.

THROUGH THE PAGES OF MY BOOK
YOU CAN JOIN ME FOR A LOOK
COME AND SEE FOR YOURSELF
THE WORLDS YOU CAN FIND UPON A SHELF

Garnet Mahaffey

(Mother of Dianne Gonzalez)

 Rosco
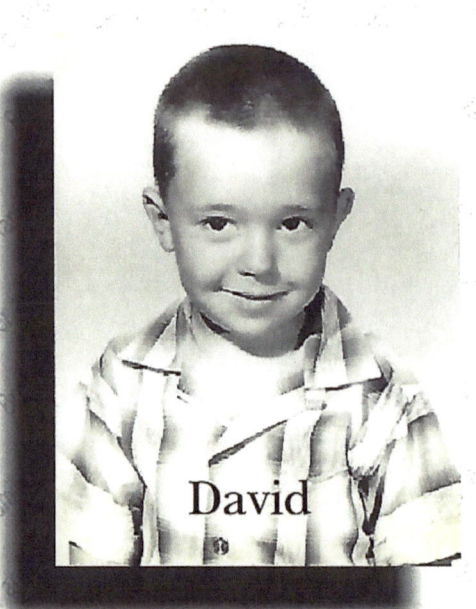 David
 Maxie
 Rosco Dianne Garnet

I remember when we were young
I followed behind you all day long
You were my big brother
You could do no wrong.

You taught me to read and write
You taught me to tie my shoe
For me, the bullies you would fight
That is why I love you.

As we grew to be adults
We went our separate paths
You into the army to fight
I, to the Capitol to type.

Both of us were wed, children did ensue
But over the years we kept in touch
Through all the times so rough
But nothing has changed my love for you.

We are both growing old and gray
As we exchange this world for another
Hopefully to see a better day
But never a better brother.

My Brother

By Garnet Mahaffey

A Beautiful New Baby Has Arrived

Look at Me!

Name Brittani Shannon Anderson
Date May 25, 1994
Weight 7 lbs. 1 oz.
Length 20"
Parents Stephanie Mahaffey
JP Anderson

Dianne

March 6, 1948 you arrived
With eyes of brown and curly hair
From your birth much pleasure I derived
You were my darling so fair.

Dianne was chosen as your birth name
But cookie was the one you answered to
Being the first granddaughter was your claim to fame
Your grandmother chose that name for you.

But childhood is long in the past.
Adulthood, marriage and children did ensue
The nickname cookie did not last
But forever is my love for you.

A daughter is a rare jewel indeed
You have one, you should know.
Also, a Son to help fill the need
And set a mother's heart aglow.

My wish for you is happiness
All the days of your life
For you I could wish no less
Than years and years without strife.

By
Garnet Mahaffey

Dinner

By
Garnet Mahaffey

The table is set, the silver laid
Shining in the flickering candle light
I haven't seen him in a decade
But he is coming to dinner tonight.

We have had many dinners
So long in the past
But today I am the winner
I have heard from him at last.

The door bell rings and I panic
My heart is all a flutter
I hope he is still romantic
My long lost lover.

As the candles burn near the end
The smoke above them hovers
Old times now are new again
He is once again my lover.

Dreams

Last night as I was wrapped in slumber sweet
In my dreams visions of you did creep
We were oh so young and gay
Frolicking like children at play.

We romped in a green meadow
Then we were running in the snow
Throwing snow balls at the stars
Hoping to hit Jupiter or Mars.

We gamboled along the Milky Way
Stopping at each star to play
That our love would forever be true
That there would always be just me and you.

I awoke with a start to find
That the days of youth are left behind
I am here on this earth and you are gone
Now you walk among the stars alone.

By Garnet Mahaffey

Earthquake

By Garnet Mahaffey

The news came on TV of an earthquake
The location was the west coast
My whole body began to shake
Thinking of the one I love the most.

Years ago you went from me
To California your fortune to find
San Francisco was the city to see
Never thinking of the love you left behind.

For days I watched and listened to hear
For any news of you
You called today to ease my fears
But you never said I love you true.

Just knowing that you are alive
Makes my heart glad
If only our love could survive
This world would not seem so bad.

Eidolon

By Barnet Mahaffey

As I walk the lonely halls of my mind
I think I see an eidolon
I look again only to find
It is your picture I gaze upon.

I never thought I would believe in ghosts
But as I travel life's streets and byways
I see your image behind each post
Why are you haunting all my days?

I loved you all the days of your life
Then you had to go from me
All I have now is this strife
And your haunting memory.

I pray your image to exorcise
I cannot go on living with an eidolon
If someone could be so wise
Please show me how this could be done.

Now that you have gone to that land above
Please let go of me
I will meet you there my love
And together we will spend eternity.

Family

While working on my family tree
I began thinking of what family means to me
My home was loving, caring place
Filled with compassion and grace.

Mother was the ruling force
Her strength came from an inner source
She ruled with an iron hand
But taking a kind and loving stand.

Dad was the one who would provide
For the necessities to survive
He worked hard all his life.
For his family to be without strife.

My siblings and I agree
That we had a wonderful family
Mom held us to her breast
And Dad was one of the best.

Now that both Mom and Dad are gone from me
I hope they have found a place in God's family
And when my time comes to an end
That all our family will be together again.

By Garnet Mahaffey

First Choice

Where oh where is my true love
Just where could he be
Every night I pray to God above
That he will return to me.

He left me oh so long ago
Just for a little while he said
Where he is I don't know
He left shortly after we were wed.

We had planned a life so full
Houses, Boats and children too
How could he be this cruel
To leave me alone and blue.

If he is within the sound of my voice
I wish he would return to me
I love him so, he is my first choice
With him I want to spend eternity.

By Garnet Mahaffey

Hell and High Water

Loving you is like riding the waves
Of a dark and stormy sea
One moment you take me high upon a mountain top
The next I am as far down a I can be

I have known heaven on earth
Happiness beyond belief
I have also been to the depth of hell
Searching this world for some relief

And you my darling, are the cause of it all
Loving and leaving is your forte
I only have you for a little while
I don't know why you cannot stay

Maybe in the future world
The sea will be calm and blue
Our spirits will soar above it all
But through hell and high water, I will stand by you

By Garnet Mahaffey

HURRICANE

The warnings were broadcast
The hurricane was on its way
Houses boarded up and made fast
Time to go, we could not stay.

The waves were crashing on the beach
Winds blowing debris all around
I watched out of reach
As our house came tumbling down.

You got in your car
I got in mine
We had hoped to go far
And leave this destruction behind.

When I reached our rendezvous
You were not to be found
I searched everywhere for you
Calling your name out loud.

Days and weeks have gone slowly by
Where oh where can you be
Every night I pray and cry
That someday you will return to me.

BY GARNET MAHAFFEY

*The pleasure of your company
is requested
at the marriage of
Sandra Dianne Melnick
to
Richard Dean Vincent
Saturday, the fifth of May
two thousand and one
at six o'clock in the evening
The Bel Air Banquet Room
12100 West Center Road Suite 320
Omaha, Nebraska*

reception will immediately follow the ceremony

MARRIAGE

Marriage is a beautiful union between two lovers
Both parties have to be kind and forgiving
If you are friends to each other
Your life will be rich and fulfilling

Dianne, Love Michael with all your heart
And I am sure he will love you too
Then you will never be torn apart
But united with a love that is true.

Michael, you know that I love you like a son
So be kind and loving to this daughter of mine
A beautiful jewel you have won
Who will stand by you through all time.

When things look dark and dreary
bring out these words I have written to you
You may be tired and weary
But in sad times they will see you through

As these nuptial vows you take
If you remember these words of mine
A beautiful marriage you will make
To endure until the end of time.

By Garnet Mahaffey

My Lady Fair

Where are you my lady fair?
Why have you gone from me
The lady with the golden hair
No more your countenance to see.

I thought our love was secure
But I turned and you were gone
Along the path of love you found a detour
To leave me lost and all alone.

My lady fair I have searched for you
All though May and December
The sun burned and the cold winds blew
A worse time I can't remember.

Will you please return to me
A life without you I cannot bear
This is my fervent plea
Come back to me, my lady fair.

By Garnet Mahaffey

My Lost Love

By Garnet Mahaffey

Last night I watched the moon in full eclipse
I watched alone as the earth's shadow crept inch by inch
Thinking of all the nights we stood side by side
Watching together while the moon the night sky did ride.

I know that I will never watch another eclipse
Because it reminds me of your sweet lips
I still remember that last kiss
Never again will I know such bliss.

But those days are no more
I have been alone score upon score
Your face I see in my dreams at night
Your body I hold so tight.

But dreams are never real they say
I have to awake to the cold light of day
Knowing you are gone from me
Never more your face I will see.

Someday in the great beyond
I will see your face in a golden pond
If there is life in another world
We will be together again, love of mine.

Retirement

After all the years as a rate clerk
I found I was really a jerk
Working my fingers to the bone
For the barest of necessities to own.

One day I said. "take this job and shove it
Because I have had enough of it
To Florida I am leaving today
The rest of my life to stay."

In Pinellas County I settled
Clearwater to be exact
My friends thought I was rattled
But who cares how they react.

My life is one of leisure
The weather you can't compare
No snow or ice to freeze you
While you tan your derriere.

The sunsets on the beach
Are something to behold
All of this was out of reach
Up north where it was cold

Now that I am here, I never want to leave
I know that someday my race will be run
But Florida will receive me
If and when I return

By Garnet Mahaffey

Sanibel

Have you ever been to Sanibel?
A barrier island in the Gulf of Mexico
There are beaches where you can tan au natural
If you get a chance you should go.

There is a lot to see on this isle
Wild life and vegetation abound
Alligators, Turtles, Ospreys and Reptiles
These and more can be found.

The beaches are lined with shells
There is also a lighthouse to see
There are churches that toll the bells
For vacationers like you and me.

If you go to Sanibel
I hope you have lots of fun
Gather lots and lots of shells
And soak up all the sun.

By Garnet Mahaffey

Silent Love

Why do we keep putting off
Things that should be done today
Now your love I have lost
Somewhere along the way.

I loved you in silence all those years
Always keeping low-key
Hoping that you would ease my fears
And declare your love for me.

But now that time has past us by
You are only ashes in the wind
My darling, at night I cry
Praying somewhere we will meet again.

I believe in a life re-incarnate
And my darling so did you
In the next life I know our fate
Will be a love brand-new.

By Garnet Mahaffey

Sunrise

By Garnet Mahaffey

As I awake to greet each sunrise
I long to see the love light in your eyes
remembering the nights we lay side by side
Planning our lives to coincide.

But fate did intercede
Our country called and you flew away
I waited years for your return to me
Each night I prayed, I prayed.

Time has sped away
The sun still rises each day
But in your eyes I will never see
The love you once had for me.

Sunrise now means just another sunset
Life is slipping away, But not yet
One day the end will be near
I am still waiting for you dear.

I have a lovely daughter named Stephanie
She means the world to me
September 11, 1958 she did appear
To her mother there is none so dear.

When she was young she was a brat
But as an adult she has outgrown all that
She grows sweeter day by day
And I love her more than I can say.

Over the years she has grown to be
A lady of which I am proud
Now my daughter Stephanie
Could stand out in any crowd

As I get old and gray
Waiting for that better day
I know that there will always be
My sweet daughter named Stephanie.

Stephanie

By Garnet Mahaffey

Today I received a letter
I Thought it would be good news
But when I opened up the letter
I got a new case of the blues.

My darling has left me forever
He wrote me a Dear John
He has found himself a new lover
And from his life I am gone.

This letter leaves me without hope
I have loved him since I was a teen
Without him in my live I cannot cope
My life is over it seems.

But all of my life I have been a fighter
Knowing this, I will survive
I will make a life that is brighter
With a new love by my side

The Letter

By Garnet Mahaffey

THE MAN I AM LOOKING FOR

I saw a face in a shop window
I thought I had seen that face before
I was ready to turn and say hello
But I realized that is not the man I am looking for.

I see your face many times within a day
I know it must be a hundred or more
But every time I have to say
That is not the man I am looking for.

I dream of you day and night
My mind is in an uproar
Each time I awake in a fright
Not to find the an I am looking for.

I know that someday the time will be
That I will open up a door
And standing there I will see
The man I am looking for.

By Garnet Mahaffey

The Masked Ball

Last night I attended a masked ball
Hundreds of people dancing on the floor
Everyone masked, costumed and all
But I found your eyes from the door.

I knew right then and there
That you would be my destiny
I was walking on air
Hoping with you to spend eternity.

At the stroke of midnight
Everyone was asked to unmask
To dance with you was my delight
And in the glow of your eyes to bask.

I have been looking for you for years
Traveling near and far
Now I have no more worries or fears
We will hitch our love to a distant star.

No more masks will we need
Now that our lives are entwined
Other lovers will recede
As our love grows divine.

By Garnet Mahaffey

The Phone

I pick up the phone as it rings
Hoping it is your voice I will hear
But disappointment is all it brings
Some one else's voice is there.

I wait and wait by the phone each day
Hoping that one day you will call
Why oh why did you go away
I don't understand at all.

I lie in bed night after night
Dreaming of you and I together
But I awake at first light
And find this day is just like another.

Someday I know that phone will ring
And you will be on the other end
No one could know the happiness that will bring
For me to hear your voice again.

By Garnet Mahaffey

TOO LATE

I learned today of your demise
My heart broke right in two
It has been years since we would devise
Ways to meet in our rendezvous.

I was married and so were you
Our moments together were stolen bliss
I hated each time we said adieu
Never knowing when there would be another kiss.

I always thought that one day
Our love we would consummate
That there would be some way
That you would be my life long mate.

But years passed and we lost touch
Out of step with fate
I love you oh so much
Now it is forever too late.

By Garnet Mahaffey

Undeclared Love

I awake at night with a start
Thinking there is someone nearby
<u>All I</u> hear is the beating of my heart
And the sobbing as I cry.

I cry, I cry, where are you my love.
Why have you left me so forlorn
I pray to the good Lord above
That you will come to me before the morn.

Many years have come and gone
Each night this prayer I pray
But with the coming of the dawn
I awake to the cold light of day.

Now I find that you have gone to that land above
Never again your face I will see
Why did we wait so long to declare our love
Which now can never be.

By Garnet Mahaffey

Walking In The Sunshine

By Garnet Mahaffey

Though the rain is pouring down
I am walking in the sunshine
Looking into your eyes of brown
Brings me happiness divine.

The winter winds blow hard and cold
But in the sunshine I walk
Around me your arms enfold
Of our love we talk and talk

The night is dark and dreary
But the sun is shining in my heart
I may be tired and weary
But nothing will keep us apart

The rain, The snow and the sleet
Are just words to me and you
What really makes our hearts beat
Is walking in the sunshine with a sky of blue

Wine and Roses

You brought a dozen roses of red
To show your love for me
Now the roses are withered and dead
But our love will always be

You brought me warm red wine
Along with the roses too
You took me out to dance and dine
As the days went by our love grew and grew

You brought me jewelry so fine
Cars, furs and houses too
Along with the roses and the wine
You kept saying I love you

You have gone away from me
And left me for all time
I think of our love when a red rose I see
And I will never again drink
            warm red wine

By
Garnet Mahaffey

Your Name

People talk and they say
That we are not right for each other
That one day you will go away
And leave me for another.

If that should prove to be true
My life would be over
Why you would leave, I haven't a clue
You have been my one and only lover.

My love for you is everlasting
I hope your love for me is the same
Please don't leave me grasping
For your love and your name.

Your name I have cherished
since I was a child of three
To marry you is what I have wished
And with you spend eternity.

By Garnet Mahaffey